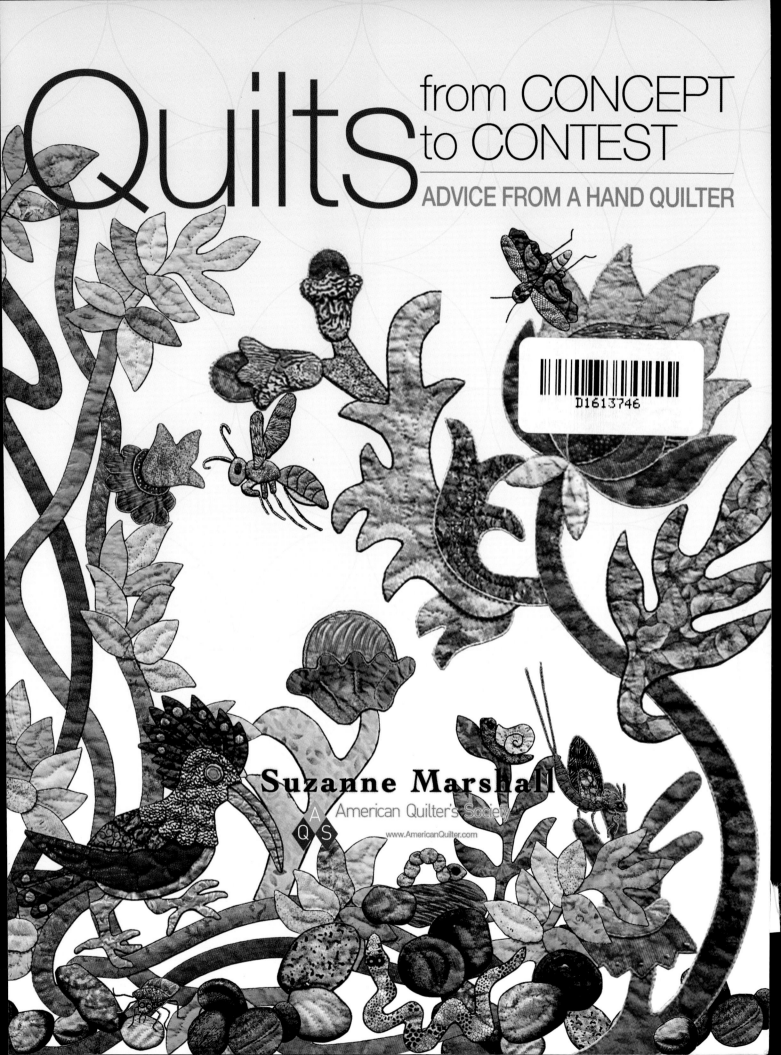

Quilts from CONCEPT to CONTEST

ADVICE FROM A HAND QUILTER

Suzanne Marshall

American Quilter's Society
www.AmericanQuilter.com

Located in Paducah, Kentucky, the American Quilter's Society (AQS) is dedicated to promoting the accomplishments of today's quilters. Through its publications and events, AQS strives to honor today's quiltmakers and their work and to inspire future creativity and innovation in quiltmaking.

EXECUTIVE BOOK EDITOR: ELAINE H. BRELSFORD
SENIOR EDITOR: LINDA BAXTER LASCO
PROOFREADER: ADRIANA FITCH
ILLUSTRATIONS: SARAH BOZONE
GRAPHIC DESIGN: SARAH BOZONE
COVER DESIGN: MICHAEL BUCKINGHAM
QUILT PHOTOGRAPHY: CHARLES R. LYNCH
HOW-TO PHOTOGRAPHY: GARLAND MARSHALL

Additional copies of this book may be ordered from the American Quilter's Society, PO Box 3290, Paducah, KY 42002-3290, or online at www.AmericanQuilter.com.

Text © 2014, Author, Suzanne Marshall
Artwork © 2014, American Quilter's Society

American Quilter's Society
www.AmericanQuilter.com

Library of Congress Cataloging-in-Publication Data

Marshall, Suzanne, author.
  From concept to contest : advice from a hand quilter / by Suzanne Marshall.
    pages cm
  ISBN 978-1-60460-166-4
  1. Quilting. I. Title.
  TT835.M27234 2014
  746.46–dc23
                                            2014040720

Contents

Why Hand Quilt?

WOW! The quilts I'm seeing in exhibits and competitions are stunning! And the vast majority are machine quilted. Most machine-quilted quilts are gorgeous, with thread painting, intricate designs, colored and varied threads, and an impressive array of artistry.

So why am I still hand quilting? I guess there are several reasons:

I don't like to be stuck in one place, tied to a sewing machine. I like to move around the house to different chairs and places while quilting.

Hand quilting is meditative and gives me a kind of peace.

I like the look and feel of hand quilting. Since we actually sleep under some of my quilts, the bed pieces that are hand quilted are comfortable and have a soft drape.

I'm stuck in an old-fashioned, traditional frame of mind.

Travel is part of my life, and I can work on my quilts in air terminals and on airplanes. I love having some handwork with me to work on wherever I may be.

It seems a waste of time to sit in front of the TV without a quilt to be working on.

Hand Quilting How-To

I hand quilt without using a frame or a hoop.

If you "rock" when you quilt and use a frame or a hoop, I guess you'll have to read another book. No one taught me how to quilt, so I came up with my own method. It's much less stressful on my joints because the hand that holds the needle doesn't move back and forth while exerting pressure to get the needle through the layers. The hand that DOES move is pinching the quilt underneath, gently lifting the quilt to the needle.

Fabric Selection

Making a decision about a background fabric that will be easy to get my needle through is the first thing that I do when starting a quilt. I actually take a needle along with some batting to the fabric store to experiment and "audition" various fabrics (with permission from the owner of the store). I learned this the hard way. A few years ago I bought fabric for an appliquéd quilt background, and when I started the appliqué, it was very hard to get the needle through the fabric. I realized that it would be even harder to hand quilt, so I went back to the store and picked a different fabric for the background.

I do the same thing when I pick a backing for my finished top. I take a piece of the fabric that I used for the background along with a needle and the batting I plan to use. Then I audition different backing fabrics. Sometimes I have to give up buying my favorite because I find one that is easier to needle.

I've learned to never buy a batik for background or backing. The weave is too dense. It is also difficult to needle a white-on-white or fabric with what looks like paint on it. Some hand dyes may be more difficult to hand quilt, but I do a lot of experimenting ahead of time in order to decide whether to use them.

Battings

It is much more difficult to hand quilt through cotton batting than the low-loft polyester or wool battings with loft. My favorite is Hobbs Poly-Down® Polyester.

Basting the Layers Together

To sandwich the top with the batting and backing, I first pin the backing of the quilt all around the edges to a tightly woven carpet. A shag rug or carpet with long loops won't work. The carpet needs to be similar to an indoor-outdoor or tightly woven Berber type carpet. While pinning the

Deruta, detail. Full quilt on page 34.

backing around the edges, stretch it so that it looks taut. Push the pins through the edges of the backing straight into the carpet and the pad under the carpet.

Next, pat the batting down on the backing, smoothing out any wrinkles. Do not stretch the batting.

Now place the top of the quilt on the batting. Stretch it the same amount that you stretched the backing and pin it through the batting, backing, carpet, and pad all around the edges. Stand back from the quilt and check to see that the lattice strips and edges are straight.

At this point the quilt is securely pinned all around the edges and it is possible to sit in the middle of it to BASTE. It is being held tightly enough around the edge to make it possible to do this. The stitches may be quite large and the direction of the stitches does not matter. You can make diagonal lines, horizontals, curves, verticals, and circles. Listen to music while basting, and dance the needle to the music in any direction.

It's highly unlikely that your quilt will be basted to the carpet. Think about how you "prick" your finger when quilting. Prick the carpet in the same way to ensure that the stitches go through to the back, but not into the carpet.

Before lifting the quilt from the carpet, remove the pins and baste in smaller stitches around the edge so that there won't be puckers when the binding is put on.

Many of my students tell me that they don't like sitting or crawling around on the floor to baste their quilt. I've had some folks tell me that they take their quilt to a longarm quilter to baste for them. This seems like a reasonable solution, although I've never tried it. Others have a remnant of carpet that they can put on a large table in order to baste. It is possible to pin it to a giant piece of foam board and prop it against a wall. The foam board could be turned in different directions as the basting is done.

Lift the quilt and turn it over, making sure that there aren't any wrinkles basted into the back of the quilt. I've never had this happen, but why not make sure?

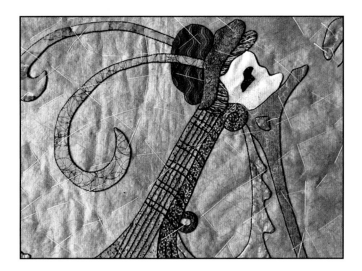

Marking the Quilt Top

If the design is really complicated and it's hard to make a template, I may actually trace the design on the top before it is sandwiched and basted. Many designs, however, such as diagonal lines, diamonds, and cables can be drawn on the quilt after the basting is finished.

Did you know that smaller stitches can be made by quilting on the bias? Is this why many antique quilts have diagonal lines and diamonds?

Ideas for quilting are sometimes found in unusual places—like tilings in a math book (see page 61)! Many quilting magazines and books have ideas for quilting designs. Even some manhole covers have designs. Architectural details, designs on fabric, wallpaper, and mosaic floors all can inspire quilting design ideas.

If the design you find isn't the right size, try enlarging or reducing it at a copy store. Golden Threads (www.goldenthreads.com) has a Quilter's Assistant Proportional Scale that "takes the math out of resizing."

It's possible to make your own quilting stencils. I like using the plastic found at office supply stores that is usually used for reports or presentations.

Experiment with markers. My favorites are the soft white Prismacolor® pencils that I buy at an art store or university bookstore for use on dark fabrics. For light fabrics I use a water-soluble pen. So far I haven't had a problem with it coming out of the fabric, although there are some bolder marks when the pen is new that need to be removed more than once.

Quilting
Where should I start quilting?
Most people think the quilting should be started in the middle. I rarely do that. The quilt is heavily basted and the layers are not going to slip. I do, however, quilt everything before I get to the border. Often I have enough quilting in the main part of the quilt that I may need to tighten up my basting stitches once I get to the border.

Beginning the hand quilting
Now the fun begins! Since I quilt without a frame or a hoop, I can drag the quilt around, moving from chair to chair, finding the best light, propping up in bed, or quilting on an airplane (if the quilt is small enough). The quilt is held together by the basting stitches better than some quilts are quilted.

To begin the first stitch, pull a knot through the top of the quilt into the batting so that it won't show on the back. Because of the flexibility of the quilt, since it is not being held tightly in a hoop, I can manipulate the quilt to meet my needle.

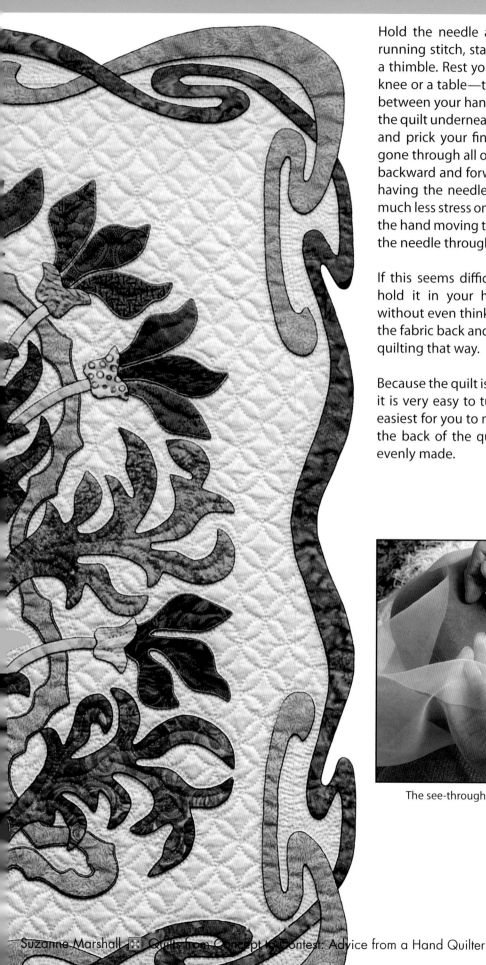

Hold the needle as if you were planning to make a running stitch, stabilizing the back of the needle with a thimble. Rest your hand holding the needle on your knee or a table—this way there can be a hoop of sorts between your hands. Then with the left hand pinching the quilt underneath, slide the needle through the quilt and prick your finger to be sure that the needle has gone through all of the layers. The quilt actually moves backward and forward to meet the needle rather than having the needle rock to make the stitches. There is much less stress on the hands quilting this way because the hand moving the quilt isn't applying *pressure* to get the needle through.

If this seems difficult, get out a piece of plain fabric, hold it in your hands, and make a running stitch without even thinking about quilting. I'll bet you bend the fabric back and forth to meet your needle. Then try quilting that way.

Because the quilt is not being held in a frame or a hoop, it is very easy to turn the quilt in the direction that is easiest for you to make stitches. It is also easy to check the back of the quilt to be sure that the stitches are evenly made.

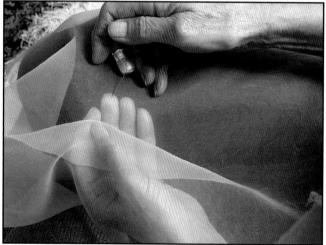

The see-through fabric helps you see how this is done.

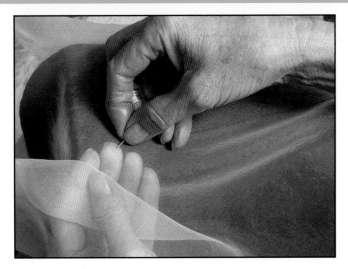

Ending the stitching

I use three different ways to end a thread.

My favorite method of ending doesn't even require a knot. If I'm quilting a continuous line and my thread gives out, I slide my needle through the batting ahead of where I will be quilting. I then try to put the needle back in the same hole or close to it to stabilize the thread along the quilting line. Move forward again on the line, moving the needle through the batting. Cut the thread off.

There is now thread in the batting right underneath the area where you will be quilting. The next quilting you do will be on top of the thread that is along that line but hidden in the batting, and it's next to impossible for it to come out. Actually, the quilting can be *started* that way, too, by coming toward the spot where the needle will start; then the quilting will be over the tail of the thread on that line.

Stabilize the needle with the thimble. Then hold the needle with the thumb and second finger to start quilting. This also helps push the needle through the layers of the quilt. Pinch the quilt from underneath, especially when you are in the middle of a large quilt.

Look up Suzanne Marshall's Appliqué on YouTube to see a video of hand quilting without a frame or a hoop. Maybe that will help. (There's also a video with an example of my Take-Away Appliqué technique.)

Another way that I end quilting is to slide the needle to a seam allowance or the edge of my appliqué. I make a backstitch there, move forward in that invisible place, and make another backstitch while hiding a knot in the batting.

My least favorite way is to slide the needle to a stitch that has already been made, trying to come up underneath the stitch. Then make a knot and make a little bitty backstitch underneath that stitch, pulling the knot through.

Practice! Practice! Practice!

Have fun! I hope this method works for you! Try quilting this way for 15–30 minutes a day for six weeks, and I'll bet you'll succeed and it will become automatic. Your hands will find their own way to work together as you practice.

Small Non-Competition Quilts:
Inspiration & Techniques
The Dragon Slayer

THE DRAGON SLAYER (2007), 20" x 67", made by the author

Suzanne Marshall ▓ Quilts from Concept to Contest: Advice from a Hand Quilter

The Dragon Slayer

Since I have been traveling around the country teaching, it has been hard to take many large quilts with me. Small quilts fit nicely in a carry-on bag and I can fit several in a checked bag as well.

Hand quilting on a small quilt is easy to do while traveling. Often interesting conversations are started when quilting while sitting in an airport terminal. The most frequent statement is, "My grandmother made quilts. Too bad it's a dying art now." That certainly gives me the opportunity to awe my fellow passenger with the high number of quilters in the country as well as the fact that it is a multibillion dollar business.

People often wonder where I get my inspiration from. For me, this comes from a variety of things! Illuminated manuscripts are fascinating to me. Finding one with a dragon caught my attention.

Uh-oh, when I started hand quilting the background, I couldn't see my stitches. I hate to admit that I resorted to machine quilting the background with stippling. But all visible stitches on the appliqué and borders are by hand.

> **Tip for hand quilting:** It's okay to mix machine and hand quilting if your handwork won't show on the background.

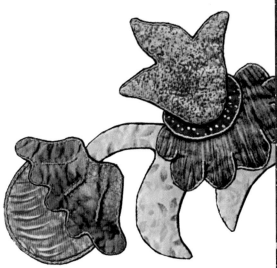

Water's Edge

WATER'S EDGE (2008), 32" x 32", made by the author

Suzanne Marshall ⊞ Quilts from Concept to Contest: Advice from a Hand Quilter

Water's Edge

A tile design by William de Morgan, the same artist who inspired the Birds quilt (page 44), caught my attention. I used metallic thread for some of the embroidery.

Tip for hand quilting: When taking a small quilt on an airplane, use small scissors with blunt ends and short blades. Revlon makes scissors that are meant for cutting baby fingernails or nose hairs. They are fairly inexpensive at the drug store, cut well, and won't be confiscated by security at airports.

Tulips on Parade

Tulips on Parade (2008), 43" x 50", made by the author

Suzanne Marshall ✦ Quilts from Concept to Contest: Advice from a Hand Quilter

Tulips on Parade

Walter Crane was a prolific British artist and book illustrator, often specializing in children's books. One of his books contained lithographic line drawings with watercolors titled *Flora's Feast: A Fairy's Festival of Flowers*, published in Britain in 1889. The drawings are of enchanting men and women dressed as flowers.

Designing the border gave me more headaches than appliquéing the center of the quilt.

Tip for hand quilting: A short needle makes it easier to quilt small stitches.

Kabuki

KABUKI (2009), 23" x 43", made by the author

Suzanne Marshall ⊞ Quilts from Concept to Contest: Advice from a Hand Quilter

Kabuki

There are many fine woodblock prints from the eighteenth and nineteenth centuries featuring actors from Kabuki theatre. The print that attracted me is of the actor Arashi Otohachi I as Numatarō Striking the Frogfish and is attributed to Ippitsusai Bunchō (1755–1790).

Tip for hand quilting: Enlarge a quilting pattern from the background for the border.

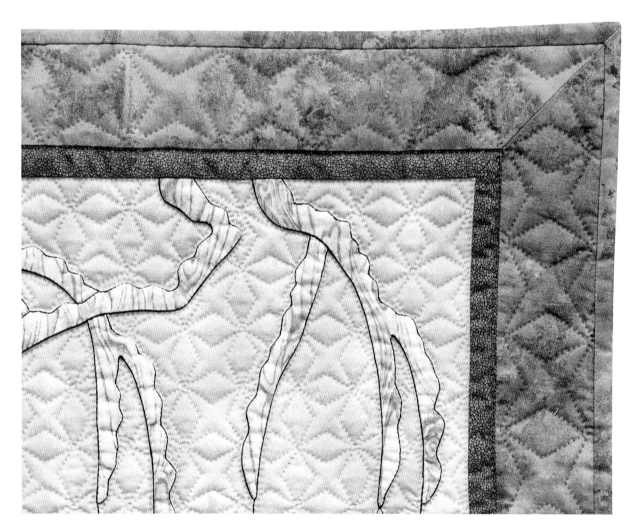

The border quilting is the enlarged pattern from the smaller background image.

The Gardener

THE GARDENER (2010), 23" x 68", made by the author

Suzanne Marshall ▦ Quilts from Concept to Contest: Advice from a Hand Quilter

The Gardener

A woodcut from 1515 attributed to Albrecht Durer's studio was my inspiration for THE GARDENER. Durer was considered the greatest Renaissance artist of northern Europe.

THE GARDENER and THE DRAGON SLAYER (page 12) have the same background fabric. So you can guess what happened! Yes, I machine quilted the background and hand quilted the appliqué and borders.

> **Tip for hand quilting:** Find a thimble that fits and stays on your finger. If you aren't used to using one, try wearing it around the house for a while to become accustomed to it.

Twisted Ribbons

TWISTED RIBBONS (2012), 35" x 38", made by the author

Twisted Ribbons

Flowers hold a special appeal on quilts. The twisted ribbons give it an art nouveau feel. The large appliqué pieces make it one of my most popular patterns.

Tip for hand quilting: Hand quilt ⅛" from the outside edge of all appliqué to hold the background down. By doing this, the appliqué will pop out with more dimension.

Suzanne Marshall ❖ Quilts from Concept to Contest: Advice from a Hand Quilter

Roosters

ROOSTERS (2013), 52" x 20", made by the author

Roosters

An illuminated Armenian manuscript known as the *Gladzor Gospels* from the fourteenth century inspired ROOSTERS. There is not, however, very much similarity between the ancient manuscript and my quilt. The roosters and urn in the center are reminiscent in shape, but the rest of the vines, flowers, and leaves were added to fill out the quilt.

Tip for hand quilting: It helps to use a slightly lighter thread on dark fabrics so that you can *see* where you have quilted.

Radiator Cover

RADIATOR COVER (2012), 81" x 11", made by the author

Suzanne Marshall 🔲 Quilts from Concept to Contest: Advice from a Hand Quilter

Radiator Cover

Our house in St. Louis is about 100 years old, built after the 1904 World's Fair. We have long radiators in several rooms. I've enjoyed making long, skinny quilts to go on top of them. Deruta pottery helped me design the dragons, although it was somewhat difficult making the beasts long and straight instead of crawling on a round plate.

Tip for hand quilting: Good light is a MUST. My favorite light is by Dazor (www.dazor.com). I have two lamps in my sewing room. One is a table lamp used by many jewelers and the other is very tall and on wheels that I can roll to the area where I need more light.

Competition Quilts:
Inspiration & Evaluations

Let's take a look at some of my hand-quilted quilts, most of which have won prizes in national competitions, and look at some of the judges' comments—both positive and negative—along with comments and observations from my husband, Garland.

The Musicians

THE MUSICIANS (2010) 67" X 41½", made by the author

The Musicians

Curious and Fantastic Creatures: 122 Bizarre Beings, a Dover publication (1995), contains copyright-free line drawings from *The Humorous Dreams of Pantagruel*, supposedly figures from the imagination of the French author François Rabelais. The weird creatures can also be found on the Internet. Be warned that several are a bit obscene, although that's really not what caught my imagination. The original book was published in 1565.

> ### *Garland's comment:*
> Rabelais wrote a series of five books titled *The Life of Gargantua and Pantagruel* that were full of crude, scatological humor and violence. As many sections were also perceived to be anti-clerical, they were suppressed at various times by the church. The woodcut illustrations themselves were not published until 12 years after Rabelais's death and are attributed to François Desprez. A likeness to the then Pope Julius II has been noted by scholars in over twenty of the illustrations.

Apparently I'm not the only one to be captured by the weird drawings. Salvador Dali, well known for his surrealist art, also adapted several of the Pantagruel drawings in lithographs, adding features to make the original drawings even more weird.

The figures are separate illustrations and not in groupings, but I thought it would be fun to combine three of the musicians together for a piece. I did "clean it up" a bit because the original drummer was really excited underneath the drum.

> ### *Garland's comment:*
> When we lived in New York, we were regulars at the Museum of Modern Art. It's possible that Suzanne was subliminally influenced by Picasso's *Three Musicians*, one of the more famous pictures in their collection.

Of course, I needed to add some bugs and a snake to make me happy. Notice the ants crawling up the singer and the snake on the drummer's hair.

Wanting to give the appearance of ground without really using grass or flooring, I found fabric with rocks that I could cut out to give the appearance of something substantial enough for the musicians to be tripping across. The rocks influenced the colors of the fabrics used in the quilt.

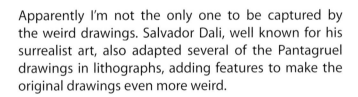

Fabric with rocks used in THE MUSICIANS

Sewing on THE MUSICIANS made me laugh!

Positive comments from judges:

*   Excellent fabric choices.
*   Black embroidery thread enhances design.
*   Reversing of fabric from border and background is very effective.
*   Use of limited color palette for this pictorial quilt is unique and well handled.
*   Embroidery and quilting stitches very well done.

Negative comments from judges:

*   Thread used for appliqué should not be visible.

Tip for hand quilting: Cut the background out behind the appliqué so that it is easier to hand quilt. Hand quilting through multiple layers is *hard*!

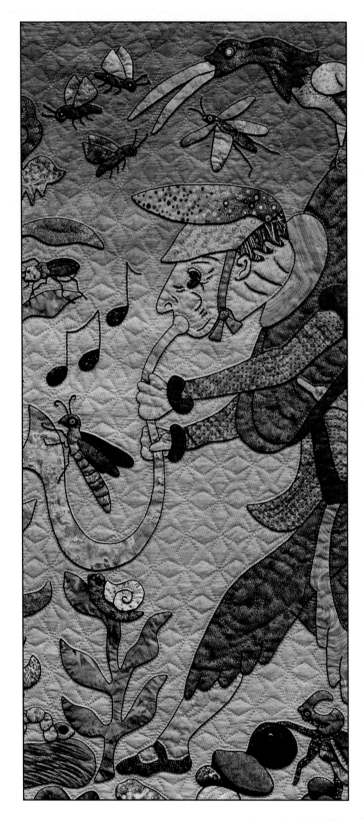

The Birders

THE BIRDERS (2011) 67½" x 43", made by the author

The Birders

It was so much fun making THE MUSICIANS I decided to select three more strange figures from *The Dreams of Pantagruel*. Adding more birds and bugs made the sewing even more fun. Luckily, I had another piece (oh woe is me, only half a yard) of fabric with rocks on it. Once again, like with THE MUSICIANS, the colors of the rocks helped me select compatible fabrics for the quilt.

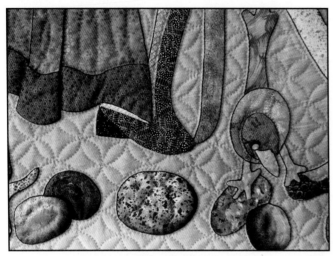

Fabric with rocks for THE BIRDERS

Positive comments from judges:

- Humorous and strong composition.
- Excellent use of shaded background fabric.
- Beautiful appliqué and embroidery technique.
- Outstanding hand quilting.
- Borders are well chosen.
- Love all the critters and especially their eyes.
- All workmanship and design well executed.
- The whole story line is incredibly funny.
- Can find nothing wrong with this whimsical quilt.
- Choice of fabrics for rocks well chosen.

Negative comments from judges:

- Batting should evenly fill binding.
- Use of lint roller would benefit before exhibiting.
- Even stitches in quilting on the back need improvement.

Tip for hand quilting: Take a needle and a piece of batting to the fabric store to experiment and "audition" different backing fabrics in order to find one that is easy to hand quilt through. My guess is that the shop owner will be happy for you to do this, but ask permission first.

Suzanne Marshall 🔲 Quilts from Concept to Contest: Advice from a Hand Quilter

Deruta

DERUTA, 73½" x 82", made by the author

Suzanne Marshall ⬛ Quilts from Concept to Contest: Advice from a Hand Quilter

Deruta

Garland has had several invitations to teach and lecture in Italy over the past several years. We have visited Deruta several times, a town that is well known for its hand-painted pottery. Many of the designs used in the ceramics have been passed down for centuries. We have purchased a few dishes and love using them.

Garland's comment:

Deruta is near Perugia in Umbria, Italy, and the small workshops there do exceptional majolica pottery as they have since the Middle Ages. Many of the designs have very grotesque, ornamental arrangements of arabesques with interlaced garlands including small and fantastic human/animal figures, that have captured Suzanne's imagination. They were used by Raphael in many of his decorations in the Vatican.

Garland's comment:

William de Morgan was the most important English ceramic artist of the Arts and Crafts Movement, a contemporary of William Morris. Suzanne fell in love with his images during a visit to the Victoria and Albert Museum in London. De Morgan's animal designs were derived from his detailed knowledge of medieval illustrated manuscripts and partly from his vivid imagination—another link to Suzanne's interest in folk art. His tiles inspired Suzanne's earlier quilt AND DRAGONS, TOO.

Going through the pictures that I took of some of the hand-painted pottery while visiting shops, I thought it would be fun to feature some of the beasts from the pottery on quilt blocks. Not having quite enough beasts from my photographs, I adapted some beasts from drawings of ceramics made by William de Morgan. He worked in the late 1800s as a tile designer in England. The blocks were a little plain using only beasts, so I added flowers, leaves, and vines adapted from woodblocks from the *Book of Hours* (early 1500s).

AND DRAGONS, TOO, 73½" x 92" made by the author

Suzanne Marshall ▦ Quilts from Concept to Contest: Advice from a Hand Quilter

The *Book of Hours* was printed in Paris shortly after Gutenberg invented the printing press. Small woodblocks framed the text and were full of imaginative creatures. VISIONS, another earlier quilt, was based on those images.

VISIONS, 82" x 83", made by the author

I'm starting to think that I like making collages of collected images, using so many different sources for ideas for quilt blocks.

And by the way, I love making BLOCKS for quilts because they are easy to take along individually on trips. The embroidery is my "mindless" airplane work. An unfinished block is so easy to fold in a small space. That and a thread cutter, embroidery floss, and needle take very little room.

Using some of the same tilings that I used for VASES made the hand quilting more interesting to do since each block has a different quilting design. Unfortunately, there is so much appliqué that it is kind of hard to see the tiling patterns.

I tried something new (for me anyway) on the corners of the borders of DERUTA. I drew out a fancy design with a bit of help from copyright-free typographic borders, modified to fit the corner spaces. Wanting the complicated design to show a bit more than the rest of the background quilting, I used a 12-wt. Sulky® thread, slightly darker than the 30-wt. thread I used elsewhere.

DERUTA, detail. Notice the similarity of the border design to the design on the cup.

Positive comments from judges:

- Combination of jewel tones and neutrals is very effective.
- Embroidery techniques excellent and add a wonderful line to the elements in the quilt.
- A balanced and pleasing composition.
- Exquisite hand quilting.
- Reiteration of fabrics throughout the blocks creates unity of design.
- Good binding technique.

Tip for hand quilting: Using different colors and weights of quilting threads can add interest in a quilt.

Images from Deruta pottery were inspiration for designs on the quilt DERUTA.

DERUTA, quilting detail.

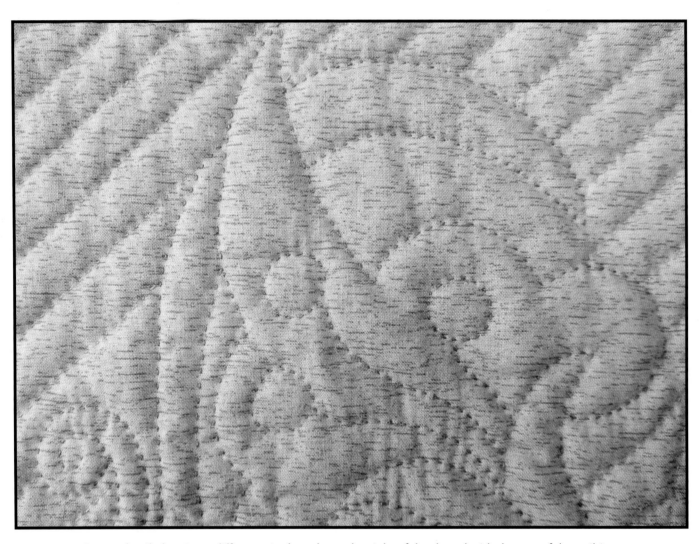

DERUTA, detail, showing a difference in the color and weight of the thread with the rest of the quilting.

Echoing Spring

ECHOING SPRING (2012), 53" x 66", made by the author

Echoing Spring

A Dover book by H. Roessing titled *2,286 Traditional Stencil Designs* has wonderful line drawings that I spent time gazing intently over for ideas for a quilt. Four designs appealed to me, so I decided to redraw them so that I could adapt them to fabric.

After finishing three and a half blocks, I became quite bored with it. After all, it didn't have any bugs, birds, beasts, or weird people to provide entertainment and make me laugh. I stashed it away, saving the pattern for the last block's blue flowers pinned to the back of my ironing board. About a year and a half later, I was really pretty tired of seeing that paper pattern still within my eyesight, so I got out the blocks again to assess whether to finish. I thought, "Well, it's not *that* bad," so I made myself go on and finish that fourth block.

Then the problem presented itself as to how to put the blocks together. I had originally thought it would be a large quilt, but it turned into a wallhanging because I ran out of background fabric. It's hard to get more fabric when a year and a half lapses while the blocks are being made.

Garland has requested many times that I use echo quilting but it just never seemed like the right piece. To make him happy, I used echo quilting around the squiggles surrounding the blocks. Then the quilt's name, ECHOING SPRING, came to mind.

Garland's comment:

The lesson is to always buy more fabric than you anticipate needing.

I was thrilled when the piece won the Coats & Clark Wall Hand Workmanship Award at AQS QuiltWeek® – Paducah, Kentucky 2013.

Positive comments from judges:

- Strength of design is achieved through appliquéd sashing in border.
- Repetition of fabric and color and shape unifies the quilt.
- Variety of embroidery for outlining defines each piece well.
- Variety of quilting motifs creates a textural background and dimension.
- Repetition of color in multiple borders frames the quilt well.
- Masterful appliqué/outline embroidery makes design pop.

Negative comments from judges:

- Miter is well achieved but light thread is distracting.

Tip for hand quilting: If your fingers underneath the quilt get sore from being pricked by the needle, try putting a couple of layers of plastic electrical tape on the sore finger.

Echo quilting in the border and the area between the blocks

Suzanne Marshall ⊞ Quilts from Concept to Contest: Advice from a Hand Quilter

Birds

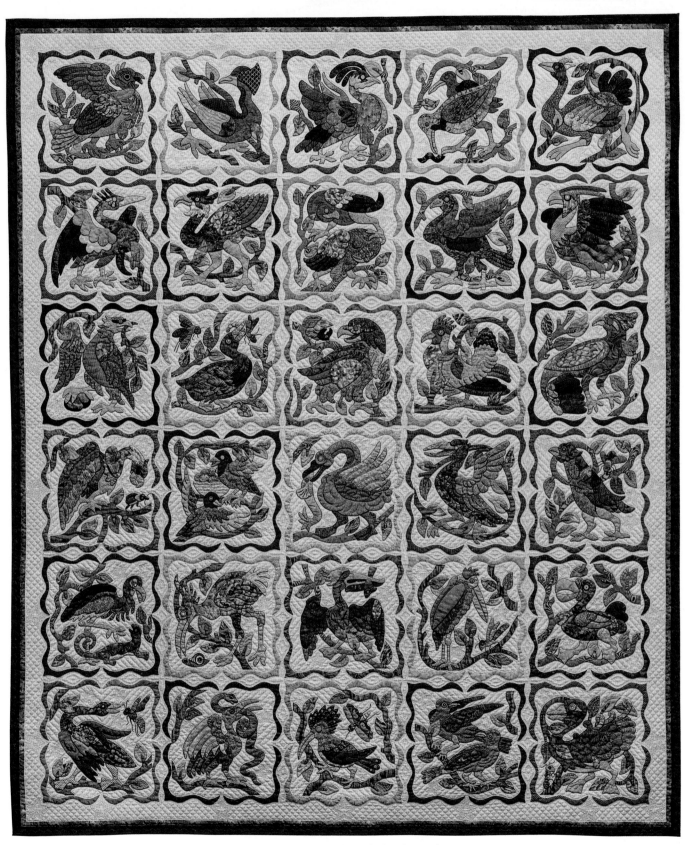

BIRDS (2013), 74" x 87", made by the author

Suzanne Marshall ✸ Quilts from Concept to Contest: Advice from a Hand Quilter

Birds

Accompanying Garland to London while he attended a scientific meeting, I spent a few days wandering around on my own and ended up twice in the glorious Victoria and Albert Museum. While there, I discovered some William de Morgan tiles.

William de Morgan (1839–1917) was a master Arts and Crafts designer of stained glass, pottery, and tiles, working in England at the turn of the century. His tiles were decorated with leaves, flowers, birds, monsters, ships, and animals. The museum shop had a book for sale with postage-stamp-sized line drawings of many of his tiles. In spite of worrying about the extra weight in my carry-on luggage, I bought the book *The Designs of William de Morgan* by Martin Greenwood (Richard Dennis and William E. Wiltshire III, Somerset, England, 1989). After emailing a question about copyright for the designs to the publisher, I was happy when I received an email reply from Richard Dennis Publications saying, "There are no copyright issues." Hooray!

Four of the bird tiles in the book that I hoped to use in the quilt had twigs and leaves surrounding them. The rest didn't, so I attempted drawing fairly simple vegetation with the birds. I think the quilt would probably be better without so many birds on it, but I couldn't seem to stop myself from making more and more appliquéd birds. Then how could I leave any of them out of the quilt?

The quilting is fairly simple diagonal lines, but I wanted to jazz it up a bit—thus, the stars quilted here and there in each block, breaking up some of the diagonal lines. I wonder if anyone will even see them!

Positive comments from judges:

- Quilting stars add interest.
- Great use of color.
- Appliqué framing of motifs very unique as well as outline embroidery.
- Love the way the eyes pop.
- Exquisite execution.
- Beautiful appliqué and handwork.
- Black embroidery pops the figures.

Negative comments from judges:

- Watch out for thread loops on top.
- I would have liked to see a few stray colors from the color palette chosen to draw eye or emphasize some areas.

Tip for hand quilting: Smaller stitches can be obtained by quilting on the bias. Maybe that's why diagonal lines and diamonds are often seen on traditional, antique quilts.

Hand-quilted star on the BIRDS

Birds, detail. Full quilt on page 44.

Suzanne Marshall 🔲 Quilts from Concept to Contest: Advice from a Hand Quilter

The Beastiary's Whale

THE BEASTIARY'S WHALE (2009), 42½" x 48½", made by the author

The Beastiary's Whale

In medieval England the manuscripts known as beastiaries contained descriptions and illustrations of real and imagined animals, fish, and birds. Along with the illustrations are stories, many of which depict morals or allegories. Since some of the creatures pictured had never been seen at the time, some of the drawings are quite fanciful and hilarious.

The illustration of the whale is an example of one of the morals told. There were men out sailing and they were hoping to find land. They thought they spotted an island, but it was actually a whale with what looked like vegetation growing on its back. They sailed over to it and tied their ship to the whale's back. They built a fire to cook some food. The heat from the fire alarmed the whale and it plunged to the depths of the sea, drowning the sailors. The allegory is that this is what happens to unbelievers.

According to the beastiary, the small fish in the whale's mouth represent men of little faith who are swallowed—the allegory being that the same will happen to those who are not firm in their faith.

Positive comments from judges:

- Everything neat and tidy.
- Miter in corners well executed.
- Exquisitely perfect!
- Beautiful handwork and dramatic design.

These comments were made when THE BEASTIARY'S WHALE won Best of Show in The Quintessential Quilt 2013 show held at the University City Public Library, St. Louis, Missouri, from October 6–November 1, 2013. This competition is the only judged and juried show in the St. Louis area and hangs for nearly a month. People visiting the library who don't ordinarily go to quilt shows are exposed to wonderful quilts, and the show has become very popular. The small disadvantage for our Circle in the Square Quilt Guild is that an admission fee cannot be charged since it is a public space.

Tip for hand quilting: Use a wooden molding strip from the hardware store to mark long straight lines. Lay it across the quilt and mark next to the edge of the wood. Line it up with the previously marked line each time for the next mark. The strips come in ⅜", ½", ⅝", and ¾" widths. Be sure it's not warped when you buy it.

THE BEASTIARY'S WHALE, detail. Full quilt on page 47.

Ceramica

CERAMICA (2013), 71" x 71", made by the author

Ceramica

Garland was a visiting professor in Rome the autumn of 2011. I spent five weeks with him there and, of course, had my eyes open for quilt-design ideas. We visited several museums including the Villa Julia and Vatican Museum that had Etruscan objects, and some of the ceramics caught my attention. The designs that appealed to me the most were influenced by Corinthian pottery from Greece. We took pictures of the pottery, and then later the next year visited the Metropolitan Museum in New York City where we found more Etruscan/Corinthian pottery to photograph.

I have to admit that most of the animals are probably from original Corinthian pottery, but I have to give Rome credit because that's where I first became acquainted with them.

Animals on the ceramics

The big puzzle for me was trying to figure out how to put diverse animals and people together in a reasonable format. That was truly a struggle.

I do like making quilts that make me laugh. The feet on the animals certainly did that.

Imagine my delight on finishing the quilt and finding ceramics in the St. Louis Art Museum with some of the same animals and birds that I included in my quilt. Patterns were apparently used over and over again when making ceramics centuries ago. Animals were a key design element for many Corinthian jugs.

This ceramic piece, exhibited at the St. Louis Art Museum, is from 590 to 570 B.C.

Positive comments from judges:

- Embroidered edges give added emphasis to these compelling figures.
- Appliqué and embroidery very well done.
- Striking execution.
- Quilting creates effective texture.

Negative comments from judges:

- Some larger appliqué patches would benefit from additional quilting for stability and definition.
- Strive for consistent quilting stitches front and back.
- Binding should be consistently filled with batting to the edge.

CERAMICA, detail. Full quilt on page 50.

Suzanne Marshall ▦ Quilts from Concept to Contest: Advice from a Hand Quilter

Tip for hand quilting: For intersecting lattice strips, find a design that connects in all directions.

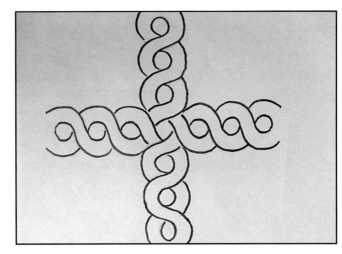

Quilting design stencil connecting in four directions

Ceramica, detail. Full quilt on page 50.

Out of Tune

Out of Tune (2014), 66½" x 45", made by the author

Out of Tune

Time to laugh again while quilting, so back to the manuscript from 1565 that inspired THE MUSICIANS (page 28) and THE BIRDERS (page 31). My last piece of fabric with rocks once again helped me select fabrics for the characters.

Have you noticed that there is an appliquéd snake on all three of the "weird" quilts? When I was a child, my father taught me how to hold snakes that we caught in the garden. I wasn't the least bit afraid of them. I thought it was fun to pretend that a snake was my necklace.

I was in such a hurry to finish the quilt in time to add it to this book that I didn't take enough time to select a backing. I should have auditioned more fabrics, because the one selected turned out to be more difficult to quilt through. It also had a rather plain design that showed every single stitch. There were several times I felt sure that my stitches weren't going all the way through to the back. I wondered if it would be obvious to the judges if I entered the quilt in a competition.

Positive comments from judges:

- Great fabric and color choices bring this unique composition to life.
- Embroidered edge appliqué is beautifully done.
- Quilting is used effectively to support the appliqué design.

Negative comments from judges:

- Quilting stitches should consistently penetrate all layers of the quilt. (Yup! They caught it!)
- Miters on the border should align with miters of the binding.

Tip for hand quilting: Check the back of your quilt to be sure that the stitches are showing evenly. Don't be in a hurry if you can help it!

VASES:
A Treasury of Background Quilting Designs

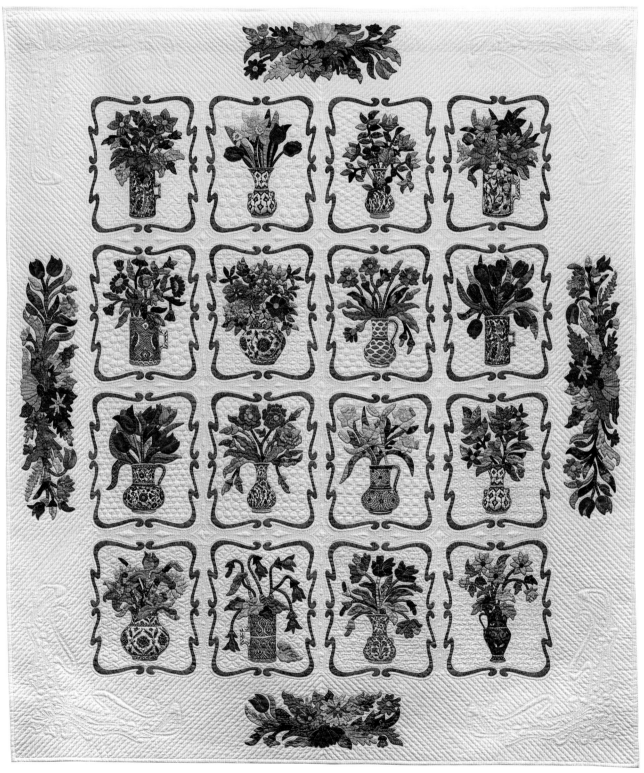

VASES (2009), 69½" x 81", made by the author

Vases

Visiting San Francisco along with my husband who was attending a scientific meeting, I had time to mosey around and stumbled upon a sort of fabric warehouse with various bolts and pieces of fabric scattered around on tables. The fabric was certainly not in any organized arrangement, and I thought it might be remnants from various projects, including upholstery.

One piece of fabric caught my eye. It was perfectly white with blue and white vases printed on it. There was nothing printed on the selvage indicating a company, but I thought it might be French cotton because there were French names printed underneath the vases.

Vases from the fabric

I bought less than a yard of the fabric. Drat! Why didn't I buy more? I stashed it away when I got home and forgot all about it. Several years later those vases "spoke" to me. I decided to try to make arrangements of flowers for each vase. I got out Dover books of copyright-free flower drawings, seed catalogs, and visited the library to look at books on flower arrangements. I spent several weeks trying to design arrangements for each vase, then started appliquéing blocks for a quilt, not quite sure how many blocks I would make, or how they would go together to make a quilt.

That hit-or-miss beginning is how I have started most of my quilts, never being sure how large they would be or how the blocks would end up living together. And the borders? Who knows! At least, certainly not in the beginning.

Around the same time my husband, Garland, gave me a big, thick book (700 pages) written by a couple of math professors. He said, "Look at this. It might give you some ideas for quilting designs."

The book is by Branko Grunbaum, a professor of mathematics at the University of Washington, and G. C. Shephard, a professor of pure mathematics at the University of East Anglia in Norwich, England. It is a treasure trove of geometric patterns. Titled *Tilings and Patterns* and published in 1987, the book is sure to be inspiration for many different fields of endeavor, including quilting!

Garland Marshall

Garland's comment:

I've always been enthusiastic about Suzanne's passion. As a scientist, the time delay between an idea, doing the background experiments, and getting definitive results can be ten years or longer. Every day I get to enjoy what Suzanne has accomplished with her latest project.

The book on tilings and patterns reflects an interest in Escher prints rather than anything mathematical.

With regard to fabric purchases, I view them as essential to her creativity; she has to find the right fabric for her expression, and she often doesn't buy enough because a given fabric has a short shelf life in the store.

Suzanne Marshall ❖ Quilts from Concept to Contest: Advice from a Hand Qu

Positive comments from judges:

- Very nice hand quilting.
- Thread outlining on individual flowers gives great dimension.
- Quilt has a lovely crisp and clean look.
- Outstanding use of color.
- Well-executed quilting enhances this quilt.
- Appropriate use of embroidery.
- Colors and fabrics well chosen.
- Excellent visual impact.
- All elements of quilt design contribute greatly.
- Use of color embroidered detail, quality appliqué.
- Variety in quilting designs adds great interest and texture to the piece.
- Outlining with thread further enhances the design in detail.
- Beautiful choice of colors of flowers on the crisp white background.
- Fabric chosen for vases is wonderful.

Negative comments from judges:

- Inside points on hand appliqué could be tighter.
- Blind stitches on the binding would make a more competitive quilt.
  (Yet it won first place, merit quilting at the International Quilt Festival in Houston where the comment was made!)
- An excellent reproduction of a popular pattern.
  (WHAT? I designed the pattern myself! Reproduction of *what* pattern?)
- We hope you continue to practice your craft at this high level of skill.
  (Okay, okay!)
- One quilting stitch did not go through to the back— just teasing. I can't think of anything to write in the "improvement" section.

As the blocks for Vases neared completion and I struggled with designing a border, I started subliminally wondering about the quilting patterns I should use. Thumbing through *Tilings and Patterns*, I thought it would be fun to try some of the tilings as quilting designs, using a different one for each block. They were complicated enough that I ended up tracing the tilings on the blocks before sandwiching the layers. It makes me laugh when I see the mathematical formulas included with the patterns.

Vases has won several national awards including best hand workmanship. My guess is that the tiling patterns had something to do with it.

Suzanne Marshall ❖ Quilts from Concept to Contest: Advice from a Hand Quilter

Backgrounds

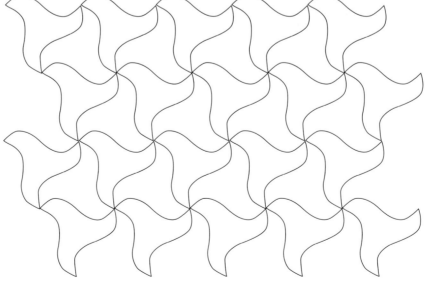

　　　　Suzanne Marshall　✦　Quilts from Concept to Contest: Advice from a Hand Quilter

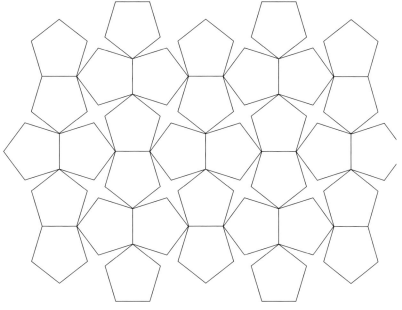

Suzanne Marshall ⊞ Quilts from Concept to Contest: Advice from a Hand Quilter

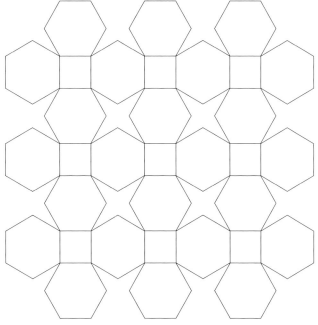

Suzanne Marshall ⊞ Quilts from Concept to Contest: Advice from a Hand Quilter

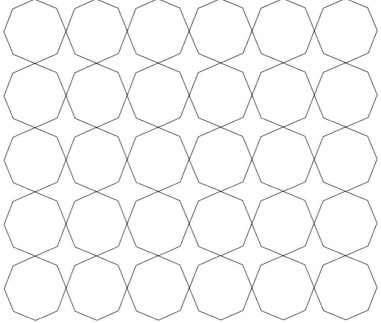

Suzanne Marshall ◈ Quilts from Concept to Contest: Advice from a Hand Quilter

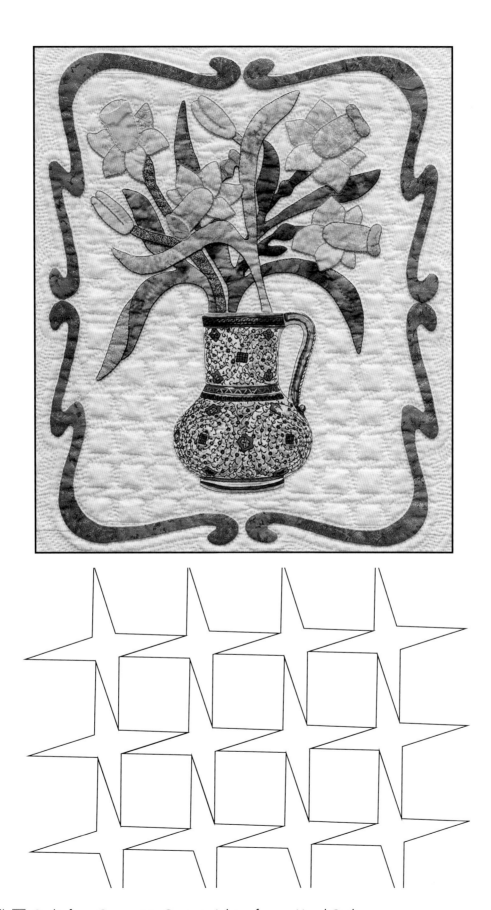

Suzanne Marshall ✺ Quilts from Concept to Contest: Advice from a Hand Quilter

Suzanne Marshall ❖ Quilts from Concept to Contest: Advice from a Hand Quilter

Suzanne Marshall ▨ Quilts from Concept to Contest: Advice from a Hand Quilter

HUNGRY BUG BALTIMORE:
A Take-Away Appliqué Project

HUNGRY BUG BALTIMORE, 16" x 16", made by the author

Suzanne Marshall ▦ Quilts from Concept to Contest: Advice from a Hand Quilter

One of the first critiques I received from judges was that my appliqué needed more quilting to provide relief. Trying to quilt through the appliqué with the background still behind it was difficult. It made sense to me to cut the background out from behind the appliqué to reduce the number of layers for my needle to go through.

After I learned that lesson, I started cutting out the background behind my appliqués. Eventually I devised a method for cutting out the background during the appliqué process. I learned that with the background gone, it helped in matching the grain line of the appliqué piece with the grain line of the background fabric. This helps maintain the integrity of the piece and helps it hang straight. All straight grains match. All bias matches.

Since I use Hobbs Poly-Down®, a polyester with loft, the batting comes up and fills the appliqué with the background gone. The wool battings with loft work, too. That gives the piece a lot of dimension. I've had folks ask if I've stuffed the appliqué, and the answer is "no." It just looks that way.

The following instructions for HUNGRY BUG BALTIMORE use my TAKE-AWAY APPLIQUÉ technique, which solves the problem of appliquéing a multipieced pattern. All the pieces fit perfectly without marking the background fabric or using transparent overlays. It also provides an easy way to control the direction of the fabric grain within the appliqué by using lined notebook paper for templates. As the pieces from the paper pattern are "taken away" during the appliqué process, the fabric appliqué pieces line up perfectly with what is left of the notebook paper.

A Baltimore album quilt by Rachel Meyer from the mid-1800s inspired parts of HUNGRY BUG BALTIMORE.

Supplies

- Background fabric square 16½" x 16½"
- Scraps of fabric for the basket, flowers, bird, leaves, cherries, and bug
- Basic sewing supplies (needle, pins, threads, thimble, scissors for fabric and paper, pencil for fabric)
- Lined notebook paper
- Foam board about 8" x 10"
- ¼ yard border
- ¼ yard binding
- 18" x 18" batting
- 18" x 18" backing

Be creative and add any kind of border that you would like. I used some green and red from the leaves and flowers.

Step-by-Step Instructions for a 16" x 16" Block

1. Press fold lines in the background both vertically and horizontally.

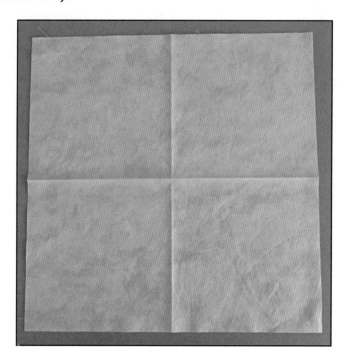

2. Measure 6½" from the middle of the block and make a small mark.

3. Mark the placement and length for the stems. These are the only marks that will need to be made on your background. Mark in the MIDDLE of where the stems will go. The marks will never show.

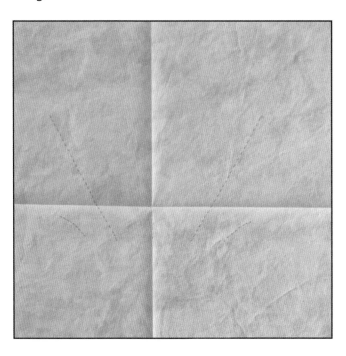

4. Trace the middle flower on lined notebook paper, keeping the paper straight across the design so that the lines on the paper are vertical.

5. Cut off the first piece to be appliquéd.

6. Pin the notebook paper template through the fabric to the foam board so that it won't slip and will be easy to draw around. Match the grain lines of the fabric with the lines on the notebook paper. Draw right next to the edge of the template. Use a marker that is easy to see.

7. Cut out the appliqué piece, leaving a seam allowance for the appliqué and a larger allowance for the part of the flower that will not be turned under.

8. Appliqué the middle stem.

9. Place the paper flower over the stem. Now it's easy to see where the top part of the flower will go, because it fits in the exact place where the paper template was cut off.

10. Baste in place.

11. Appliqué, then baste the EDGE of the seam allowance that will be covered by the next piece.

12. Cut the background fabric out from behind the appliqué piece. Leave ¼" of fabric near the appliqué stitches and cut close to the basting stitches.

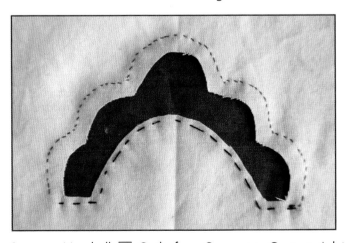

13. Proceed with the second piece of the flower, remembering to line up the lines on the notebook paper with the grain lines of the fabric.

14. The notebook paper shows where the appliqué piece goes.

15. Appliqué and baste next to the edge of the raw seam allowance.

16. Remove the basting stitches behind the first appliqué piece.

17. Cut out the fabric behind the second appliqué piece.

18. Continue with the rest of the flower, cutting out the background each time a piece is added. When you finish, the entire flower will be stitched without any background behind the appliqué pieces.

Suzanne Marshall ☒ Quilts from Concept to Contest: Advice from a Hand Quilter

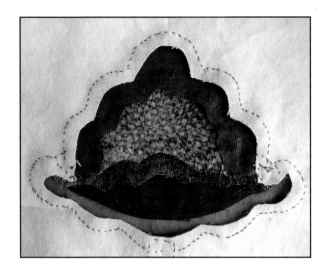

19. Baste and appliqué the stems in place.

20. Baste a contrasting fabric to the BACK of the basket fabric, being sure that it covers the cut-out areas in the basket.

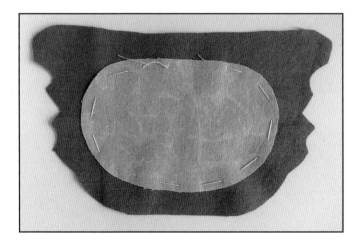

21. Complete the reverse appliqué, which is really like regular appliqué except that the appliqué stitching is done on the contrasting fabric that was basted on the back of the basket.

22. This is what the reverse appliqué looks like from the back after the gold fabric has been trimmed.

23. Add the gold part of the base of the basket before appliquéing the basket to the background.

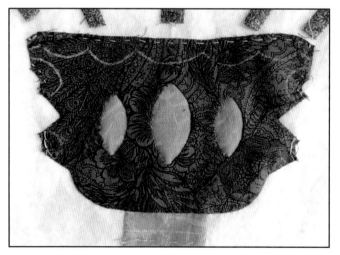

24. Don't forget to cut the background fabric out behind the basket.

25. The red flowers also need to have the background removed before adding the centers.

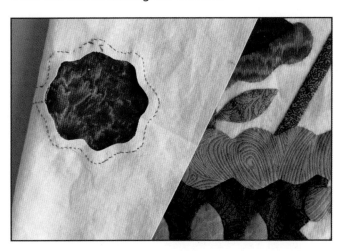

26. Embroider around the pieces to help define the appliqué from the background.

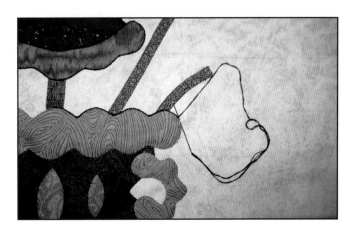

27. Try adding another row of embroidery!

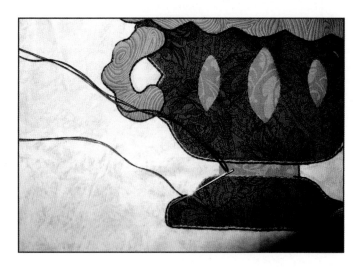

28. Use take-away appliqué for the side flowers.

29. These photographs show one flower with embroidery and the other without. See the difference!

30. Compare the front and back of the finished piece.

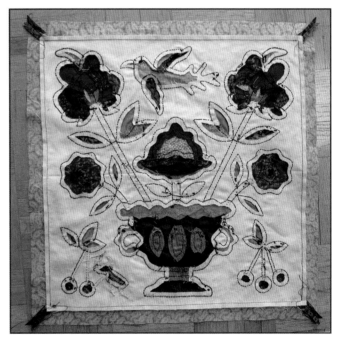

31. Square up the block. Add borders that you like using fabrics that complement the colors used in the block. The borders may vary in width and may be of more than one color.

HUNGRY BUG BALTIMORE **Pattern**

Suzanne Marshall ✖ Quilts from Concept to Contest: Advice from a Hand Quilter

HUNGRY BUG BALTIMORE pattern top left – Pattern shown at 100%

HUNGRY BUG BALTIMORE pattern top right – Pattern shown at 100%

Suzanne Marshall ⬚ Quilts from Concept to Contest: Advice from a Hand Quilter

Hungry Bug Baltimore pattern bottom left – Pattern shown at 100%

HUNGRY BUG BALTIMORE pattern bottom right – Pattern shown at 100%

Suzanne Marshall ▨ Quilts from Concept to Contest: Advice from a Hand Quilter

Meet
Suzanne Marshall

Photo by Garland R. Marshall

Suzanne started quilting in the mid-70s by checking out a library book. As a self-taught quilter, she has developed her own way to appliqué and quilt. She feels lucky to have two quilts in the permanent collection of The National Quilt Museum in Paducah, Kentucky, after winning hand workmanship awards at the American Quilter's Society Quilt Show and Contest. Her quilt TOUJOURS NOUVEAU was selected as one of 100 Best American Quilts of the Twentieth Century. She has won prizes in many competitions, both nationally and abroad.

Suzanne and her husband, Garland, live in St. Louis, Missouri, and enjoy visits from their four children and ten grandchildren.

More AQS Books

This is only a small selection of the books available from the American Quilter's Society. AQS books are known worldwide for timely topics, clear writing, beautiful color photos, and accurate illustrations and patterns. The following books are available from your local bookseller, quilt shop, or public library.

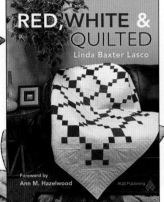

#1651

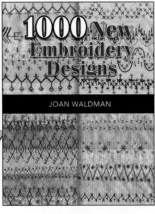

#1644

#1646

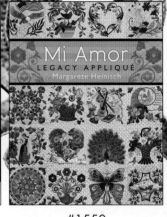

#1550

#1546

#1548

#1549

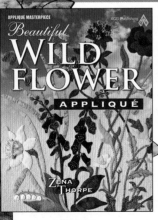

#8526

#8672